Inner Wo:
the Mind

Ashleigh Heenan

BookLeaf
Publishing

Presentation by *BookLeaf Publishing*

Web: www.bookleafpub.com

E-mail: info@bookleafpub.com

ISBN: 978-93-95890-10-6

First edition 2022

DEDICATION

In memory of Anne.

Thank you for always believing in me, I couldn't have done it without your support and friendship.

I miss you.

Who am I

I am the moon
I am the sun
I could be the stars
But that would take it too far

I am the heat
I am the cold
I could be the ice
But that wouldn't suffice

I am the water
I am the earth
I could be the fire
But that would draw ire

I am the past
I am the future
I could be the present
But that wouldn't be pleasant

I am everything
I am nothing
I am and I am not

Lost at War

The spring has sprung and summers over
Autumn passed and winters closer
The air is crisp and bitterly cold
It seems to seep into my soul

Christmas cheer is all around
I slip and slide on the ground
Loved up couples is all I see
My loved one cannot return to me

Lost, in a faraway place
Fighting for us, to be safe
This time of year, holds no cheer
I wish I was no longer here

The years go by and bitter still
My pain won't go away with a pill
Angry right until the end
Finally reunited with my best friend

The spring has sprung and summers over
Autumn passed and winters closer
The air is crisp and bitterly cold
In death together, we join our souls

Found in Death

The spring has sprung and summers over
Autumn passed and winters closer
The air is crisp and bitterly cold
It cannot seep into my soul

I am gone but never forgotten
I fear her soul is slowly rotting
I wish for her peace of mind
To her life, she is so blind

She wishes to be free from life
It causes me so much strife
I fought so hard for a better world
Especially for my girl

A life so wasted she could not see
She always had a part of me
But for my love, I will wait
And welcome her at the gate

The spring has sprung and summers over
Autumn passed and winters closer
The air is crisp and bitterly cold
In death together, we join our souls

Echoes

Echoes of my mind
Echoes of my heart
Echoes of a past, I thought I'd left behind

Echoes of a different time
Echoes of another place
Echoes of a pain, that is fully mine

Echoes of all I've known
Echoes of the things I've loved
Echoes of the memories, that are mine to own

Despair

A life well deserved is a life lived well
Except when life is a living hell
The very depth of my soul is broken
My torment and shame will remain unspoken

My darkest days remain with me constantly
Never a breather, my demons are persistently
Chasing me through this world
How have I never yet learned

I cannot be free to be happy and relaxed
This will only end when I am axed
My life is over and I should surrender
I thought we were forever but he was a pretender

When I leave this life by my own hand
He will know that this was planned
I have to do this to be free
And find my resting eternity

Emotions

I have a fear
It controls my mind
I have a fear
I can't leave it behind

I feel anger
It consumes me
I feel anger
I want to flee

I feel confusion
I want to hide
I feel confusion
It fills me inside

I feel sadness
It will not pass
I feel sadness
It continues to harass

I feel surprise
I'm no longer dead inside
I feel surprise
There is a turning of the tide

I feel relief
I am blessed by change
I feel relief
Life no longer feels strange

I feel joy
It seeps to my soul
I feel joy
I am more in control

Reflection

Why does my reflection not look like me?
Is this the image that the world can see?
Who am I, if not what I imagine
Can I change this, can it happen?

Am I pretending to be something I'm not?
Is this the real me or something left to rot?
Does my reflection, reflect the real me inside
Should I be going out of my way to hide?

I used to see a different picture
Now it's like I'm a different fixture
To who does this image belong
Is it the real me or still so wrong?

Why does my reflection not look like me?
Is there a difference that we can agree?
Who am I, if not what I imagine
Please show me some compassion

Guardian Angel

As I slipped underwater
I felt as if I was drowning
My life flashed before me
It was truly astounding

The messes I've made
And the relationships burned
I need to make amends
So, I have to return

An Angel appeared and told me
That I must get it back
This needs to be fixed
Take the time, I can give you that

I came too and felt such relief
The Angel was gone, but I had work to do
The mistakes of the past must be undone
I must make it right and start anew

My family comes first and I must confess
I was such a brat and misunderstood,
Took out my teenage frustration on
Those I loved and need to make it good

We reconciled and I am so happy
I have a new lease on life
Now I will be the best I can be
And cause my family no more strife

Wherever you are Angel
I can't thank you enough
You have saved me from
A lifetime of rebuff

I have mended my ways
and my life will improve
I hope you will be watching
And I pray that you approve

Autumn

The leaves are swirling
Reds, browns, greens
The colour of Autumn

The time of change
Of seasons moving
A new beginning

The ground is crisp
And the air is brisk
I quicken my steps

Embracing the new
Fighting the winds
Living in the now

Drowning

Treacherous, as the leech who betrayed you
Furious, the feeling upon learning of the betrayal
Turbulent, the relationship had its moments
Sullen, the betrayer after being found out

Ominous, the feeling something wasn't right
Relentless, the pursuit of seeking the truth
Tempestuous, the anger you will reign down
Perilous, the danger of the end

Endless, the feeling that this is forever
Mysterious, how could this have happened
Distant, the signs were there all along
Everlasting, what you thought you had

Sombre, was this all I ever wanted
Hypnotic, cast under a fake spell
Incredible, a learning experience
Mesmerizing, in its own tranquil way

Deep, as the feelings in the beginning
Calm, as you learn and move on
Majestic, each new one gives hope
Hungry, for a more fulfilling life

Imaginary Friend

I met a young girl when I was small
People said she didn't exist, only in my mind
But, she was the one that was there for me
She helped me a lot when I was a child

I never cared that she wasn't real
It felt more real than if we were sisters
I cared for my friend with every fibre of my
being
And I know that she cared for me too

Why else would she be standing there now?
As I am about to bring my child into the world
The child that I will name after her
My very real and imaginary friend

Memories

As I stare at the old photograph
I wonder what became of the people
Did they live a happy life together?
Or did fate intervene and change their path

She looks so young and vibrant
Full of life and happy as can be
He looks so handsome and alive
Full of love as he looks at her

I ponder on the idea if they had kids
Raised a family and thrived in this world
The photo appears to be old
Do they perhaps have grandchildren?

Faded memories whisper across my mind
I am broken out of my musings
By the door to my room opening and
A woman, I'm not sure I know enters

She spots the photograph
Smiles sadly and asks how I am
I feel like they had a good life, I say
I can promise you that they did, Grandma

The Fortune Teller

My beau and I went to the fair
And found a fortune teller there
Her face lit up all aglow
How much is this, I wanted to know

I couldn't hear what was being said
The look on my girl's face filled me with dread
She came out and ran past me crying
I caught up and convinced her, she's probably
lying

Later that week, it all started to come true
Is it because it was fated or because we knew?

If you and your beau go down to the fair
And meet the old fortune teller there
Be careful and pass her right on by
Or you could just kiss your life goodbye

My Friend

You never let me runaway
You taught me to stay and fight
I had to learn how to handle
This thing called life

You made me stronger
You taught me to be bolder
It's a shame that you
Will never get any older

Wherever you are
I will never forget
You were my friend
I am glad we met

I Remember

I danced with the devil in the moonlight
I tangoed with an angel at sunset
I swung with a demon at sunrise
And when I look up to the skies, I remember

I met Santa for a coffee in the Winter
The Tooth Fairy preferred tea in the Summer
Me and Cupid chose wine in the Spring
And as the seasons change, I remember

The Troll and I went to the cinema
I met with a Fairy for a late dinner
I sung with a Gnome at karaoke
And when I go out with friends, I remember

I've met with Ghosts, Ghouls and Goblins too
However, the Wizards and Witches were new
The Centaurs and Dragons were hard to take
Meeting the Gods may have been a mistake
And when I wake up, I Remember

Is this Love?

If you fall I will catch you
My heart is full of fire
Your smile makes me weak
I am filled with desire

You shine like the stars
In the night sky
I dream of forever
This is the best high

We belong together and always will
My life is to be forever by your side
Home is wherever you are in life
Together and forever we will be tied

If you fall I will catch you
My heart is full of fire
Your smile makes me weak
I am filled with desire

The Old Fisherman

His face appeared to be carved in stone
His eyes looked into my very soul
He looked at me with his cold steel gaze
It was almost as if he was in a haze
He stared out into the deep stormy sea
It was as if he looked straight through me
I wondered what his story told
He looked to be a thousand years old

Fire

Choking,
On the thick black smoke
Blistering,
Heat all around the room
Seeking,
Sanctuary from the burning
A fiery hell of my own making

Solitude

Wilderness
Remote
Emptiness
Alone
I live for the quiet

Solitary
Recluse
Secluded
Hermit
I crave the solitude

Confession

I whispered into your ear
If only you could hear
You were gone too soon
On a summer afternoon
I fell into a deep depression
I loved you, was my confession

Words

The words you look for
Won't come to mind
You have to search
Your heart and soul

Are they hiding?
Are they there?
Do they want to be found?
And spoken aloud

Can you recall
The words to say
And express yourself
In your own way